Acknowledgements:

I would like to give honor, and thanks to God for being the head of my life and the orchestrator of this book. I would also like to thank my loving husband, Antonio, my brother Zaire, sister Alicia and Pastor for pushing me to get this done.

Table of Contents:

God's Adoption

Brought into this world, premature by three months
Mother, intoxicated with drugs while pregnant with her
She was never given the time to even "know" her
Mother, fought, but lost the fight to keeping her child

Never seen her, until that visit... still young
She was adopted, and saved by God, given
the family that was necessary for her growth
Nourishment, and support...

When she was young, she didn't fully comprehend "adoption"
She knew, someone took you in and loved you, but it wasn't your
biological family, she knew, it was safe and okay to do anything
around
these new people... what she didn't know, was that it was God's
Adoption......

God's Adoption, was the act of him behind the scenes of her life...
making sure she is still okay, until this day.... It was God's
Adoption...
that allowed her to meet the people she knows today and use her
experience
not to sadden others but expose others to the goodness of God...

God's Adoption.......<3

Not Made to Be Hurt and Afflicted

Being violated at such a young age…
Not knowing the consequences, it might bring
Told Shhhhhhh… Don't tell…. not knowing the wage, it may
bring her in the future...

Time and Time again…. It happens
Heard that Shhhhhhh. Don't tell… please don't tell…
Keeping it on the inside and putting it in the back of her mind.

Baby girl, that was the past and here you are. Renewed in me…
I brought you out so u can be a testimony…
Don't be ashamed my daughter…

You were not made to be hurt and afflicted.
Used and Abused… Violated and taken advantage of.
That's why you're my daughter.
Daughter of the King… Daughter of the King of Kings
The people that took advantage, was once in their life inflicted
with the same thing and they brought it on to you…

Baby girl. I need you to understand… you were not made to be
hurt and afflicted. Used and Abused…. Violated and taken
advantage of…
You're my daughter…. And I love you and I will forever and
continue to restore your innocence and build you up…so you can
be a walking testimony.

I love you. And You were not made to be hurt and afflicted.
But loved and adored. given hugs and kisses. And shown that
unrestricted, everlasting love. The love I bring…. I am with you
baby girl… My daughter. Remember… You're a Daughter of the
King, the King of King

Perspective of A Heart

Ouch, as her heart beats. It's as if a dagger has just stabbed her chest and the pain is coming full force. Her heart has been trampled, stepped, abused, and used and misused until it felt worthless. Tears can't heal the wounds of hurt that has congested this poor heart with barely a beat left. Carrying the burdens and troubles of others as if she was the deliverer of all problems, but her own. She failed at realizing that her heart never belonged to those who said they loved her, who touched her softly and gave her lips kisses. They didn't care like Christ. Jesus Christ, he picked up his child and used his mighty power to remove each wound person by person, being delivered and set free from the hurt. Today she doesn't wear her heart on her sleeve for those to borrow or buy for misuse or abuse. She holds it close to her chest knowing that Christ is sitting within and that he is constantly making her change from sin to righteousness.

This is a story of a girl named change.

My Love for Him

Without his love, life is like a beat that you cannot follow

My love for him is so pure

As he speaks to me in Apollo

His righteous ways makes me lure

It's so real! I can feel it in my heart

As the day goes by I still love him

I know for the future we will never depart

Because these feelings are just the start

So I love him, love him, yes I do

As I stress it in this poem even more

I love Jesus! , I think you should too

A Breath of Fresh Air

I can breathe and finally release what I have been holding on to
for so long.
It seems as if it was so hard, but now that I have let it go, the new
beginning will flow.
It is a breath of fresh air, filling my lungs and through my nose it
goes.

The burden is gone, and God is good, for I finally gave it to him
to keep.
I will not go back, think back, or even pick it up again, because I
gave it to HIM.
HE is the author of time, the beginning and the end...... and
everything in between as well.
I can spread my arms, and let out a true laugh, because the
shackles are off and I refuse to retrograde back into my past.

Thank you Lord for what you have done, so far for me.
Words cannot describe or I cannot even begin to utter the feeling
you have given to me.
Thanks for saving me, from me and my past. My prayer is that
this feeling of a breath of fresh air will last, just like you.

"Reflection"

So God created mankind in his own image, in the image of God he created them; male and female he created them.

But in the fall we lost our image

Our self-image became distorted, convoluted & destroyed to believe a misconception of who you're not.

Confused in your mind which is a battlefield. opposing two ideas of who you are in Christ and what you see in the mirror. This is where action takes place.

TAKE your image and Give it to God and let Him melt it down

You will then see Him, and yourself in another image, another light, a new reflection.

You will NEVER be who God called you to be until you give up YOUR reflection, your image of who you THINK you're supposed to be.

Don't THINK when we have a God who KNOWS.

How to Love Me

Love is the light breeze that blows on a summers day.

Ever so delicate but not pushy.

Show me you care by telling me how much you think I'm beautiful and how lucky you're to have me...

not every so often but for me to know

 that you still choose me & me alone.

A Piece of Me

If bedrooms could talk, they would speak of bent knees
and quiet prayers
The day you left, I wasn't aware but I could tell
something wasn't there
Now that you're gone, my heart, mind and soul must
move on because time is supposed to mend the pain
Time is supposed to heal, they say but those are lies that
lips speak and a cliché that never seems to be
Only true healing comes with work and acceptance
But as I sit and write, the only reason you have come to
mind is because of my life
When you've reached the point of no return, you accept
the next phase
I began to think of the fallen tears and broken hearts that
would've happened if the news hit their ears...
the crying cycle would be inevitable, but it would soon
end because in time we must move on
As you are the missing piece that I wish still exist.
I thank God I am not the same piece from
which your heart may one day miss

Bright Smile

When you cry yourself to sleep and feel nothing but pain it should be hard to smile, but it's not for her because that's where she hides. A smile so bright it takes away the questions and distracts the mind from the inner core values of what's behind it and if it's genuine. Coming from the soul to the body to the physical, a smile. She hides behind her smile because that's where she finds security in knowing that her burdens will forever choke her and her silent cries will never be heard because her smile shines brighter than bright stars and never gives doubt that something could possibly be wrong. There's no crookedness or no half smirk that could signal that something is going on but its full and there and you would not even dare to look straight in her eyes for they tell lies that pillows are dry and that the house is peaceful and that she loves the presence of her family...

But when you cry yourself to sleep at night but have a smile that's bright you can seep through the cracks of no one realizing how close to death you really are....

~@hidesbehindhersmile

Out of Sight, Out of Mind

Mental pictures of us being together rack my brain because right now you're out of sight but not out of my heart, every beat was the sound that I depended on for guidance. Entangled with your love, I was trapped but never afraid or doubtful about getting lost in you because that's where I wanted to be. You were always there and your soft words spoken in my ear and whispered to my heart are distant memories of how your love felt. I cry not because I'm sad but because I am lost and I can't seem to find all my pieces. The phrase "get it together" has become so disdained in my mind because I'm trying but failing and dying with kindness. Like my heart is outside my chest and it still beats for I am still alive as I hold it in my hand with the chains that bound my hands and my feet because you're out of sight so you're out of my mind but never from my heart which holds the beat to where you will guide me to my identity and fix me again to be the woman you see as your daughter, as your conqueror...

Count The Cost. Choose LIFE (Prayer)

God help me to count the cost before I say yes to a commitment. I am praying for maturity to pause, to ponder to ask questions... Is this life or this death? I am praying for us to take responsibility. Don't let the enemy allow us to do the blame game. I ask that I take on the sacrifice that comes with life, the prosperity that comes with life.... I thank you Lord for allowing me to no longer subconsciously choose death because nothing good comes from death. Lord allow me to make more informed and better choices. Allow me to be more confident in my choices I make for you. I shall be confident and steadfast in my LIFE choices. My choices of life shall be planted by water I pray that my choices of LIFE shall bring life. I pray that the enemy cannot persuade, cannot deceive me, pull me or deter me to making the wrong choice. I thank you Lord for the choices I make today with the relationships I have in my life and will not be a negative one but will be a sound choice. Lord I pray that you will pull me back when I am making my choice. When I make my choice, I am firm and steadfast in my choice. I speak boldness. I have to learn to defend my choice and stand up for my choices. You don't have to explain everything to everyone... THIS TIME I WILL STICK WITH MY CHOICE. I will stay confident in my choice. I CHOOSE LIFE. I CHOOSE LIFE NOW. Amen.

Once you choose life, everything that has to deal with death has to go from your life. I choose life and I refuse death.... I can't die because I refuse death in my life.

Isaiah 43:19

Behold,
I will do a new thing; now it shall spring forth; shall you not know it?
We cannot decipher the season because of the pressure within
God spirit cries: "Do you see, what I see? *singing*
Distorted by the perspective of sin, we don't. God we don't
I want to... I need to, we need to, get it together, because the time is NOW
God's calling and it won't stop until we surrender and bow!

Behold!
I am doing a new thing!
He is calling us to come UP and come OUT of the ordinary and rise above our limits
He is asking us to SEE and RESPOND to His hand of preparation in our lives in the
Church- His Bride
Are you expecting God to do a new thing in your life?
Rivers of living water will brim and spill out on anyone who abides by His dream
God will redeem, because He is the supreme one!
So I leave you with this... much is on the horizon, much lies ahead...
BELIEVE in yourself again, BELIEVE in YOUR dream... God can prepare us, but we need to partake to ACHIEVE.
Credit: lines 10-12 came from a devotional

Miracle

I'm in need for a miracle...

something that surpasses my understanding of the
struggle I need to be taken away....

I'm in need for a miracle...

only my father, my savior, protector, provider, my I
AM..... can give.

I'm in need for a miracle...

to remove me from ME and give me him. a renewing of
my spirit in HIM.

I'm in need... I'm in need.... I'm in need.... I'm in need of
a MIRACLE!

something that surpasses my understanding of my
struggles that needs to be taken away.

I'm in need of Him.

M-Miracle Worker. I- I AM. R-Redeemer... A-Almighty.
C-Caregiver. L-Love. E-Edifier

M-I-R-A-C-L-E.......

Stuck Between Myself and A Hard Rock

I'm stuck.... Can anyone help me?
Lost in this mind of mine... don't want to try no more
I give myself away and for what? His love.
Whose love? His Love. God's Love.
But I'm stuck between myself and a hard rock
You can get out... How? When?
I've put myself through the same stupid things
How can I get out this one? When because this storm
Seems like its forever and a day.... I'm stuck
I'm stuck between myself and a hard rock.
Can anyone help me out? Anyone?
Okay... maybe not. I got to get myself out
Out of this storm... You need an umbrella and a rain
coat
And some rain boots.... Hmm that's not the storm I'm
talking about
Well I'm stuck and I can't get out... Looks like I cannot
bring about

A conclusion to my disillusion of being stuck between
myself and A Hard

Rock............

The Tree

If you think about it, you're a tree
Now it depends on what kind you are…

Are you the Oak tree?
The Cedar, Cheery or Elm?

Maybe the Magnolia or the Maple
Or even the Pine or Willow

Well whichever one you are they have
One special thing in common…….
They are all trees that can endure…

In their winter times, spring times,
Autumn years, and their good times
Which are their summer times...

Soo Are you the tree that can stand strong
And have your feet implanted in this earth or in
Other words... the word of truth…. Or Are you the
Tree that falls when there is a bad storm or when the
Wind is just a little too hard for you to handle…

Well figure out what tree you are…. and if you're the
one
That easily staggers and falls… get some Miracle –
Grow which
Is the Lord Jesus Christ… and Let's Go... Just get
back up again

Life is Brick Wall

Life is a brick wall
Blank, hard, and not easy to penetrate through

Life is a brick wall
There is only one way to overcome it, which is, to go
around it

Life is a brick wall
If you cannot stand the toughness, you will begin to fall

Life is a brick, just a brick wall
You know when you can't do it alone….

Life is a brick wall
Once you look at the facts.

Life is a brick wall… but you know what else
God made life and the brick wall

So he is the big truck, that can hit this struggle down
And see you not with a frown but with a smile on your
face.

Soo just to let you know, your struggle is your brick
wall...

Are you using your big truck which is God to let it down?

Original Teenager

I am not the original teenager you see day by day.
I am not the original teenager you see dancing to Hip-Hop and laughing away.
I am not the original teenager because God changed me from being a copy to being an original.
I am not the original teenager that goes to parties and have sex and drink.
I am not the original teenager to lust upon a R& B rapper or singer or any man of that sort!
I am not, just not! the original teenager. But God did place me on this earth to be me and stay his original copy.

My Aunt's Song

I remember as if it were yesterday she was here
She would tell me how nice I looked
Sometimes I wish I was there but all I could do was shed
a tear
It was just so sad, it took me by its hook

I remember as if it were yesterday when she called my
house
Her voice so calm, like everything was fine
But everything not being good worried her spouse
She loved her children which was her shine

For she loved everyone which was great
We loved her so much it was like a glow
We all knew so much about her, which was a lot on her
plate
After all, it was wonderful having her here seeing her
grow

But My Aunt's song sings in my head
Making me remember all the things she said

R.I.P. Aunty G

All Glory To God